CHOCOLATE

That's how they make it!

Elaine Moore

Troll

This book is dedicated to
chocolate lovers everywhere!

The author and publisher would like to thank the following:
Hershey Foods Corporation, Hershey, Pennsylvania,
for their courtesy, enthusiasm, and assistance in this project;
and Scharffen Berger Chocolate Maker, San Francisco, California,
for generously providing photos for this project.

Cover photography and pages 26, 28 by Steven Dolce; pages 3, 17, 19, 28, 29
copyright © Elaine Moore; pages 4, 5, 6, 8, 20, 22, 23, 24, 27
reproduced by permission of Hershey Foods Corporation;
pages 7, 9, 10, 11, 13, 15 courtesy of Scharffen Berger Chocolate
Maker; pages 12, 16 copyright © Troll Communications L.L.C.

Pillsbury Frosting Supreme used with permission of The Pillsbury Company;
Betty Crocker Brownie Mix used with permission of General Mills.

Mmmm, chocolate. Chocolate candy. Chocolate cake. Chocolate chip cookies and hot-fudge sundaes. We eat these yummy treats every day. But where does chocolate come from?

It all starts with a special bean that comes from the cacao tree. The cacao tree is so delicate it will grow only near the Equator. There the climate is warm all year round. Different varieties of cacao trees are grown on small farms and huge plantations in countries such as Brazil, Ghana, and Trinidad.

The pods, or fruit, on the cacao tree are really peculiar. The pods don't hang from the tree, like acorns or apples. Instead, they grow right from the tree's trunk and main branches. Twice a year workers chop the ripe pods off the trees. Other workers open them with sharp knives called machetes. Inside each pod are twenty to forty pale yellow beans. These beans don't look, smell, or taste anything like chocolate. But they will!

cacao pods

Next the beans are placed in wide trays. A thick covering of burlap or a layer of yellow banana peels is laid over the trays to keep in the heat. When the beans get hot, they start to ferment, or ripen. Fermenting will help bring out the chocolate flavor.

After three to six days in the fermenting trays, the beans no longer have a bitter taste, and they have turned from yellow to purple to a rich, chocolatey reddish-brown. Afterward, the beans are dried in the sun or under huge fans to prevent molding. Only the beans that are clean and healthy will be shipped to chocolate factories. There they will be made into cocoa powder, baking chocolate, or chocolate candy!

cacao beans

8

When these very important beans arrive at the chocolate factory, they are sorted and washed. Then they are blended. Because there are different kinds of cacao trees, there are different kinds of beans—each with its own special flavor.

Every chocolate factory has its secret recipe. A certain number of this bean and a certain number of that are blended to produce that factory's particular chocolate taste. That's why your favorite chocolate always tastes the same each time you bite into it.

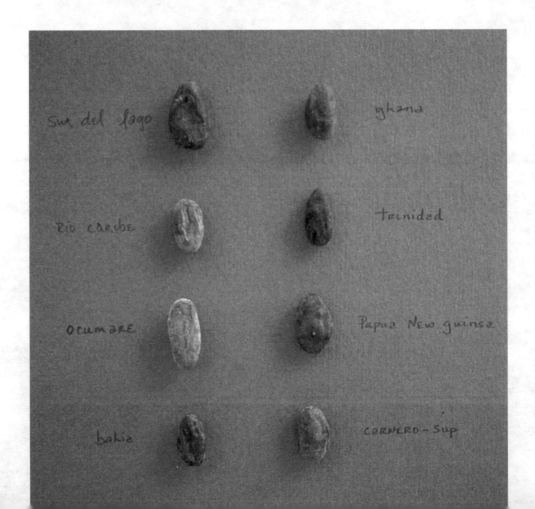

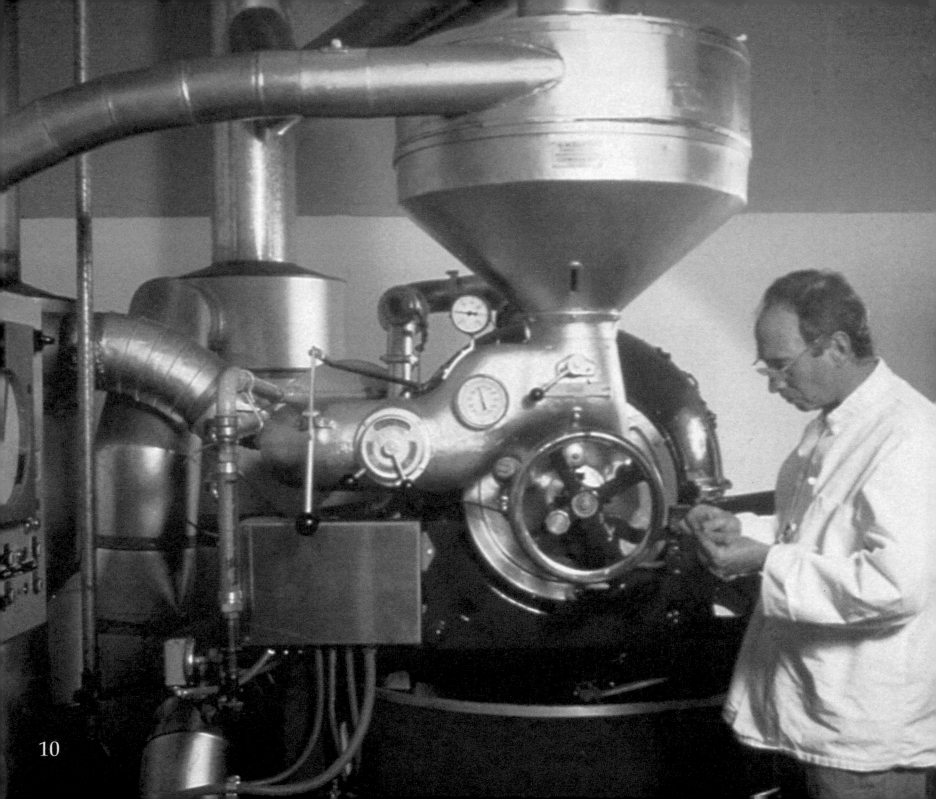

After the beans have been blended, they're roasted. Some factories roast their beans in machines that go around and around like a gigantic clothes dryer. Other factories send their beans through a sweltering tunnel on a conveyor belt. Either way, the beans get really hot. When this happens, the delicious aroma of chocolate fills the air. Mmmm!

Quickly the beans are cooled and moved to a winnowing machine. It would take forever to shell cacao beans by hand. That's why the winnowing machine is so fantastic. With great gusts of wind, this huge machine blows the cacao beans against a steel plate. The shells crack and blow up, up, and away.

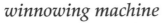
winnowing machine

roaster

All that's left now is a tiny piece called a nib. The nib is the most important part of the whole bean. That's because nibs contain cocoa butter. Without rich, fatty cocoa butter, we couldn't make real chocolate.

But what do you do with a bunch of nibs? Well, if you work in a chocolate factory, you grind them with stones and steel. This turns the nibs into a heavy liquid paste called chocolate liquor, which is mostly cocoa butter.

But wait a second! There still isn't enough cocoa butter in chocolate liquor to make the kind of candy kids like to eat. What happens next?

nibs

nib-grinding machine

The chocolate makers separate the chocolate liquor into two batches. Then they take cocoa butter out of one batch and add it to the other. This sounds simple, but it isn't. The chocolate makers must first store the chocolate liquor that won't have the cocoa butter taken out.

How do they do this? By pouring the chocolate liquor into rectangular molds. The chocolate liquor cools to form blocks of unsweetened chocolate. These blocks will be wrapped, stored, and used later for baking—or for making candy.

But remember, we still need to get the cocoa butter out of that other batch of chocolate liquor!

unsweetened chocolate blocks

cocoa cake

Workers pump this batch of the thick brown paste into a huge hydraulic press. This monster machine squeezes cocoa butter out of the chocolate liquor.

At the same time, something else happens. When all the precious cocoa butter has been removed from the chocolate liquor, what's left is round, dry, and hard as a brick. It's called a cocoa cake, but it's not the kind of cake we'd want to eat! The cocoa cake is ground into cocoa powder. It will be used for baking treats like brownies and for making hot chocolate.

Thanks to a bunch of tiny beans and some huge machines, we have cocoa powder, cocoa butter, and unsweetened chocolate. We'll need even more special machines before the chocolate is made into the chocolate candy we eat. But for now, these three important products can be wrapped, packaged, and sold to grocery stores, bakeries, and candy manufacturers. Then they will be made into all sorts of sweet, gooey snacks!

Did you know it takes two, four—or sometimes more—days just to make one candy bar? Think about that the next time you buy one!

The chocolate candy we eat is mostly a mix of chocolate liquor before the cocoa butter is squeezed out, sugar, and extra cocoa butter. Creamy milk chocolate uses these same ingredients, along with milk solids. Of course, other tasty ingredients might be added, too. Remember those secret recipes?

But whatever the recipe is, the process is the same. The extra cocoa butter, blocks of unsweetened chocolate, and sugar all need to be mixed together. The mixture is melted, then it's moved to a large mixing machine. At this point, the chocolate is as sticky and grainy as cookie dough.

mixing machine

Once the ingredients are fully mixed, the chocolate travels through heavy rollers until it's blended into a smooth paste. These big rollers are called conchers. Conching really brings out the chocolate flavor. The conchers work back and forth through waves of chocolate in a big stone tub. The friction of the waves slapping against the stone heats the chocolate to between 120 and 190 degrees Fahrenheit (49 and 88 degrees centigrade). The conchers can move slowly or they can speed up to whip air into the chocolate. It all depends on the recipe. The recipe also says whether the conching should last for several hours—or several days!

conching machines

23

Some chocolate factories don't use conchers. Instead they use a machine that looks like a giant eggbeater to make the chocolate mixture silky smooth.

But no matter how the chocolate is blended, the next step is always the same. The melted chocolate is poured into molds. Special ingredients—such as nuts, raisins, or crispy rice—are dropped into the molds after the liquid chocolate.

The molds are set on a long conveyor belt, where they are bumped and rattled to shake the air bubbles out of the liquid chocolate. If the air bubbles weren't removed, they would leave holes in the cooled chocolate.

Next, the molds are rushed through a cold tunnel. Hooray! The liquid chocolate has hardened. At last, we have candy bars!

chocolate bar molds

Chocolate manufacturers are careful to keep their factories clean. They run many tests to be sure that each candy bar is pure and tastes exactly right. Wouldn't you like to be a taste tester?

After the candy bars are checked, they travel to a packaging room. There, the bars are gently eased from the molds. Right away, super-fast machines begin scooping them up, turning them, and wrapping them in shiny foil. Next, the candy bars are slipped into paper wrappers. Workers check the wrapped chocolate before it moves on to the packing room.

More machines gather the wrapped candy bars and shoot them onto trays. Workers put the bars into cardboard boxes. Then the chocolate bars are shipped to stores, where they are bought by people like you and me.

Wow! Chocolate!

How Chocolate Candy Is Made

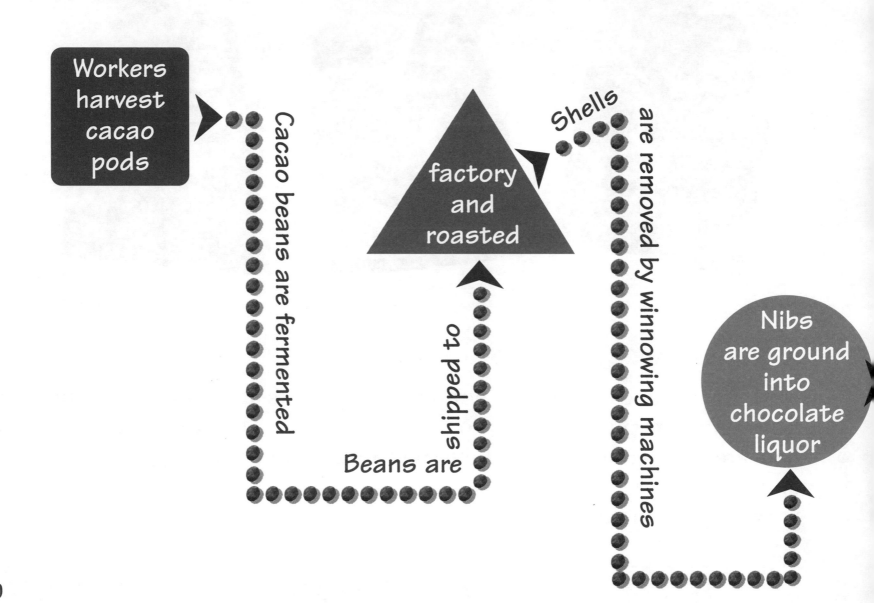

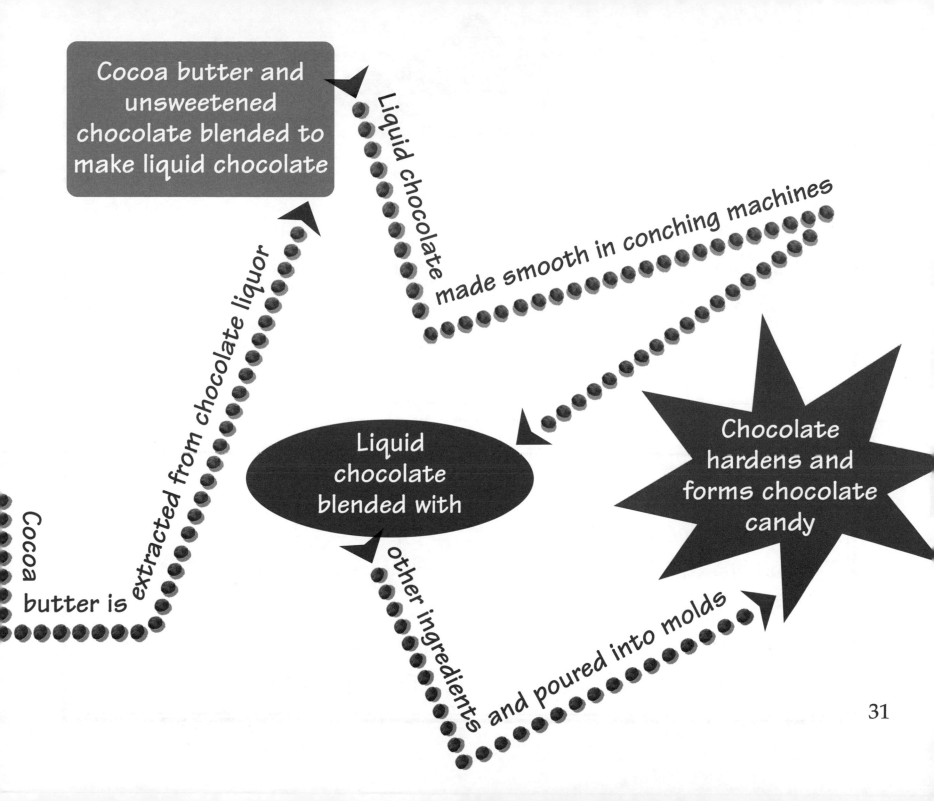

Cocoa butter and unsweetened chocolate blended to make liquid chocolate

Liquid chocolate

made smooth in conching machines

Cocoa butter is extracted from chocolate liquor

Liquid chocolate blended with

other ingredients and poured into molds

Chocolate hardens and forms chocolate candy

Index